SONG TITLE SERIES

COUNTRY WOMEN

FEATURING

ANNE KIRKPATRICK

TANIA KERNAGHAN

FELICITY URQUHART

BECCY COLE

MELINDA SCHNEIDER

KASEY CHAMBERS

JOAN MAGUIRE

Copyright Page

New Country Women

Author: Joan Maguire

National Library of Australia Cataloguing-in-Publication – Publication entry

Author:	Maguire, Joan.
Title:	Country Women / Joan Maguire.
ISBN:	978-0-9808551-5-9
Series:	Song title series.
Subjects:	Country Women
	Country Women (Country Singers)
	Australian Country Singers--Australia--Biography.
	Country Singers--Australia--Biography.

Dewey Number: 782.421642082

Published with the assistance of Love of Books and is available through the Print on Demand network and www.songtitleseries.com

This book is also available in a large print or E-book format.

The original soft cover short story book was created and written by Joan Maguire on 26th November 2010 ©
ISBN: 978-0-9808551-5-9

E-book re-written May 2014© and is available through providers listed on www.songtitleseries.com.
EISBN: 978-0-9925964-2-2

The large print book was created in March 2015 © and is available through the same distributors as the normal book or www.songtitleseries.com
ISBN: 978-0-9943297-1-4(large print).

DEDICATION

I would like to dedicate this book and say to thank you to my Earth Angel David and his friends, who inspire and motivate me to achieve things that I never dreamt, were possible.

INTRODUCTION

This time I challenged myself by using six different Australian country women singers, Anne Kirkpatrick, Tania Kernaghan, Felicity Urquhart, Beccy Cole, Melinda Schneider and Kasey Chambers as their songs and their styles in writing were all different. It doesn't matter how many times a song has been played at different times; the title is used that many times in the book and not just once.

Legally I can not use Lyrics or Music because of Copyright but I can use song titles and due to the nature of my books; legally I must place a Reference and Bibliography in the back of the book. The pictures of two of the artists on the cover were supplied by the artist's management and are mentioned in their Bibliography.

A combined total of 739 song titles (Italicized) have been used to make this story about six women of different ages who are invited to a park for a funeral with each woman believing they are there for the funeral of an acquaintance from their past, that they have personally known. But are they right?

They are greeted by a man called James and are asked to wait as there has been a delay in the proceedings. As the women are standing around waiting for the funeral to start; a conversation begins that gets each of the women to recall memories of their past with either family or friends. When it's time for the funeral to start, another man appears who has no idea who James is, when asked by the women.

What is the real reason for their meeting and who was the person who invited them to the funeral? Who is James and what is involvement in each of the women's lives?

When reading this "Song Title Series" book, I hope that no disservice has been done to the artists as well as their adoring fans who read it, for that was not my intention. As I may have missed a song, an album or a concert within this book I do apologize sincerely.

So, sit back, relax and enjoy the reading and don't forget; because I have used the original song titles in whole, there are places in the book that I could not change to make it more comprehensible for you the reader.

ACKNOWLEDGEMENTS

I would like to thank my daughters, Jenny and Kylie for their positive but critical input in the first draft of this book and all the help and support that they given me throughout the Song Title Series books.

I would also like to thank my son Peter and his family for their support and help in keeping me grounded.

I would also like to say a special thank you to Colin and Beth for their help; especially when it came to the country living sections.

I would like to thank Kay and Julie for their patience and understanding whilst teaching me and giving me the skills to present my unique books in the best way possible.

I would like to thank the artist's management for supplying the pictures for the front cover.

Thank you everyone else who has helped me bring this book to life and to you for buying it.

OTHER BOOKS IN THE SONG TITLE SERIES

CONTENTS

Title Page

Copyright Page

Dedication

Introduction

Acknowledgements

Other Books In The Song Title Series

Chapter 1 Memories   2

Chapter 2 Love and Lies   9

Chapter 3 Men and Women   15

Chapter 4 The Mystery Man   20

Chapter 5 Second Chances   26

Reference

Kasey Chambers   34

Melinda Schneider   39

Beccy Cole   42

Felicity Urquhart   46

Tania Kernaghan   48

Anne Kirkpatrick   49

Bibliography   55

About The Author   56

Testimonials   57

MEMORIES

"Ah! Anne, Beccy, Kasey. Are you three ladies the only ones coming?" said James as he walked towards them.

"No; look here come Tania, Felicity and Melinda walking up the path now." said Anne.

"Good." said James "We can get started in ten minutes; I know that you all knew him and he would have liked to have been here to see all six of you together."

"Hi girls." said Kasey "I'm glad that you could make it too. I know that we all have busy schedules but it's really something that he wanted; all of us together for a short while."

"I know." said Tania "Although I didn't know him very well, I re-arranged my day so that I could be here now."

Kasey said "*These pines* remind me of my *old school* and the *one more year* that I had left to go.

It was *Christmas time* and the *old man down on the farm* made me a *paper aeroplane* to put all my troubles on, so I could fly them away and a *monkey on a wire* to make me laugh. The only trouble was the *monkey on the wire* didn't work and the only time I was really happy, was when I rode my *pony, Rattlin' Bones* in my back yard, the *Nullabor, the biggest backyard* that anyone could have. We lived in one of the *two houses* near the train line and *living on the railroad* line was so noisy at times.

One day, while I was out riding *Rattlin' Bones* and singing a song that I had made up, called my *Nullabor song,* an *Australian son* of someone was driving *a stolen car* that got out of control and got stuck on the train tracks.

The six fifteen train wasn't able to stop in time and crashed into the car, causing *a train wreck* near *Jackson Hole* and just down the road from where I lived.

The driver of the car escaped injury but he was badly shaken and because he couldn't go anywhere, he stayed with us until the police came and took him away.

Before he left with the police, he said to me "You have the *devil on your back* that will make you a *wildflower* and also a *gypsy bound* to travel the *road to nowhere.*"

'Cos *the devil's inside my head,* I did become a *wildflower* and one day I rode *Rattlin' Bones* to *Jackson Hole* and jumped on a *freight train* and was *half way to Sydney* when I was caught and returned home *safe and sound.*

The *saddle boy,* Henry, was sent to *Jackson Hole* to bring *Rattlin' Bones* back home.

A year later, when I was in my final year of school, the eldest son of *Georgia Brown,* Hank, rode with me and *Rattlin' Bones* to the *dam* near *Jackson Hole* and he wanted to make *love like a hurricane.* Although I resisted, I couldn't believe that he could *love someone like me.*

It didn't last long because he had a *short fuse* and he often said to me "*Don't talk back.*"

He put up *barricades and brickwalls* and became dangerous because of his temper. I became a *beautiful mess* and used to *cry like a baby* and after I had cried a *million tears* over him, I walked out on him.

Going from *heartbreak heartmend* took a long time; however, the *wildflower* in me disappeared. Mind you, sometimes I think that he was *the sweetest waste of time* that I could have had *when we were kids* and I've also heard that *he still thinks I care.*"

"I know what you mean." said Tania "*We're a lot like each other.* When I was younger, I wanted to go *droving cattle with the boys.* They were *goin' bush* to find some stray cattle and drive them to *higher ground. Harley McTaggart,* who was aged about *30 something,* told me that my *dad's not gonna like it* if I went with them to the *big sky country,* but I did go with them; I had to *steal away* in order for me to go.

The *drovers boy* became very friendly towards me and we had some innocent fun together, until one day he said "Come and *ride with me bareback.* If you say no, *I will lasso you* and we'll have the *ride of our life* anyway."

Even though he was a boy, he had the *heart of a man* and acted *like the last great romantic* bushman.

3

He ended up being *the mongrel* by telling me "You give me *too little love*, so *don't fence me in*. I can do what I want, when I want, even go *fishin' in the dark* if I want."

Then one day he left and the *twinkle in my eye* went with him. I was young and I jumped into that relationship *boots 'n' all* but I soon found out that the *price you pay* for a *little piece of paradise* is *picking up the pieces* when it all goes wrong."

Anne said "*In the country town* that I came from, a *broken bleeding hurting heart* with a *train wreck of emotion* on the *merry-go-round of life* was common.

Everybody's looking for something on a Saturday night and I found mine one *Saturday night at the movies*. *Sad movies always make me cry*, so I still had the sniffles when I left the theatre and as I turned the corner into *Goulburn Street* I bumped into *Louise*, an old friend, who took me to the *Circle Café* for a coffee.

Out of the blue, Louise asked me what I was doing that evening and I told her that I was going to catch the *eastbound train* home and watch some telly.

"Oh no you're not." said Louise "*You ain't going nowhere* except with me. I am one of the *women of the west* and we were *born for the night life*. You can play *oh lonesome me* on *another Saturday night;* however, tonight we'll go to the *Showman's Daughter* Club to listen and dance to the *Grievous Angel* band and before long you will *feel a whole lot better*.

I used to be *Bobby's girl* but *all he did was tell me lies* and the biggest one was that he was at home with *a bottle of wine and Patsy Cline*, but it wasn't Patsy, he was with *Annie Johnson* in our *cradle of love*.

When I confronted him, all he said was "*I guess we've been together for too long* and *I'm thinking tonight of my blue eyes* and yours are brown".

My *old aunt Elisa* told me once, that *when it's lamplighting time in the valley*, don't go *standing too close to the flame* of love because sometimes from the *game of love*, you can only get *love from the sidelines*, other times, loves *hold's too strong* for you to fight.

And think rationally. You can never feel too *safe in the arms of love;* even though you think that your love could be *goin' strong, goin' wrong* on the *roulette wheel of love* can happen as well.

I said *goodbye* to Bobby and started *knockin' around* with *John Hardy* and guess what; I made *the same mistake* with *John Hardy.*

He was seeing a *honky tonk* girl as well as dating me. *All he did was tell me lies* as well, so I said *goodbye* to my *old home town* and moved to *French Waltz* Valley and I *feel a whole lot better* for doing so. *I don't go back anymore* to my home at *Peppimenarti Cradle* Station.

Tonight I'll shoot the moon in *Sin City* but if someone asks if they can *take me home,* I usually say that I'm staying with my older brother and they don't ask anymore."

Melinda had a bit of a chuckle and said "I usually say that I live in the *Black Hills of Dakota* and the only way to get there is by the *Deadwood Stage* bus line.

The story of my life has been like *Que Sera Sera* and parts of it are kinda like a *sentimental journey.*

Sometimes it takes balls to be a woman and you have to be even *stronger* to be a *superwoman,* especially *when the last child leaves home* to make their own way in this *big world, small world* depending on how you look at it.

I'm my own grandpa, because I often remember when he told me "Always *be yourself,* be *courageous, love somebody* else as well as yourself, *cry a little* but never to the point where you have *no more tears to cry,* but; remember the *healing power of helpless laughter* comes *from the inside out* to the world around us.

If you are having a *bad day, count to 3* slowly and if you have to, *count to three* again. If you still don't think that things are going to change, then *in your head,* ask God to turn your day around and the *beautiful thing* is, he usually does it. You must always remember to say *thank you* for his help."

Beccy added "You don't have to ask for help just on bad days, God grants *little victories* every day.

5

What matters most is how you act and what you do with your life, and if you *leave love out of this, life goes on* and *this heart* keeps beating.

I'll tell you a short story of mine and one of my *little victories*.

I was born in a small farming community called *Kansas City,* named after the American town of Kansas, well, my *big brother* always taunted me by calling me *lazy bones* all the time and he continually ran me down because I was one of the *big girls*.

How wrong is it for a *big brother* to be so *insensitive* and do something like that to his own sister?

Anyway, I became accustomed to the *single girl blues,* until one Saturday when I went to the carnival that had just came to town and I met Danny who was one of the *Wild Ones*.

The *Wild Ones* were a band that travelled occasionally with the carnival because they were able to play a variety of music; like the two guys *dueling banjos,* to the *Cow Cow Boogie,* but Danny; he could make his *guitar talk.*

Danny's song was *bad news for the blues,* and because he had heard that the *girls out here* love to *keep on rockin'* with each other because the *men don't dance anymore; that's the sound* he needed to make to keep them dancing *under the new moon.*

That evening, just by chance, I met Danny standing *by a fire of gidgee coals, foolin' around* with some other guys and he could *skip a stone* across the dam to the old *lifeboat* moored off shore that the townsfolk liked to swim to.

My *single girl blues* soon disappeared when he invited me to join him as he was going to the *Galleries of Pink Galahs,* a sideshow attraction that was situated at the base of the *Blackwood Hill.*

He told me that he preferred *big girls* because they were more of a *natural woman* than a *poster girl*. That night I found my *secret love.*

The following day, one of Danny's band members told me to be careful because Danny *never sees anything through* and that *guitars Cadillacs* and *his hometown* girlfriend are all that matters to him and when he's out playing, he often talks *sweet nothings* to the *big girls* he meets.

6

When I found Danny, I heard him say to the female he was with "Here comes a *storm in a D cup*." and then he walked over to me and asked me "*What's up?*" as he saw the look on my face.

When I told him about what had been said to me, he replied in a smart manner "*Sorry I asked*."

"What did you just say to me?" I asked him.

"*Sorry I asked*." was his reply.

I then said to him "*Say you love me* and *kiss me where I stand*…You can't, can you? *You weren't in love with me,* you were simply playing with *this heart* of mine, but *this time* you're going to wish that you were in *someone else's shoes,* especially when the *girls out here* in this town and other towns learn about you and your tricks. You have *some lessons* to learn; *only love can break a heart* and yours will *rest in pieces* once your girlfriend finds out about the real you."

Danny laughed and said "My girl back home is a *better woman* than you; anyway, *you ain't woman enough* to be *strong enough to bend* because *you're so square* and you live here in *Blackwood Hill* Ridge, where just the *ordinary world* goes flying by. *A wild turkey* is more interesting to catch, than *some lazy bones,* like you seem to be."

I looked him straight in the eyes and said calmly "You may insult me by calling me *lazy bones* and insinuate that I am not *strong enough to bend,* but *what matters most* is that I'm *too strong to break* and you *can't have that,* can you?

You think that you're a big man if you are able to put down a female enough to make her feel unworthy; especially in front of another female, but you'll be playing the *clown song* before long, instead of *the Tennessee Waltz.*

You may be *wild at heart* and think that you come from the *cool world* but eventually you will be brought back to the real world where you'll see that the *wild turkey, rainbows, dreams and butterflies* will be all that you'll have left to be *friends for a lifetime* with as all the other people won't want to know you."

I turned and walked away, leaving him red faced in front of the other female."

Felicity burst out saying loudly "Yeah, what a *country girl,* standing up for yourself.

That story reminds me of *Ernie's daughter;* Amber, who was a *lonely girl.* She had *old man trouble;* her father would carry *on & on* over everything she would say, do or wear.

She said to her father one day *"We'll never get along* anymore, will we? Why do you always have that *big black cloud* hanging over you? *I remember you* being so happy before *the flood* came and washed away parts of *Sugar Town* and mum.

You're *still alive* dad, and so am I, and *a little joy* every now and then would be good. Why won't you tell me why that *big black cloud* keeps hanging over your head?

Don't you think that in the past five years since mum's been gone, that I haven't been on a *roller coaster* ride as well. It's time to *live a little* dad, it's *time for change."*

Her dad gave her a strange look and replied softly "I have *too many secrets* that I can't tell you about now, but please remember; *jealousy* will only knock you off the *planet of love* if you are not careful. It changed *my life* and has taken *all good fun* and laughter from my heart.

I still love you as much as I did when you were the baby *girl in the mall* looking for Santa. One day, some *dear someone* will come and take you away and when they do, you might just as well *turn out the lights* for I will be forever in the dark."

"Don't talk like that dad." she replied and then continued saying. "Yes, one day I will leave home but you will always be here for me to come home to. You may have secrets that you can't tell me but that doesn't mean that you have to stop living. We can still do things together and have fun. How long has it been since we went horse riding together?

Why don't we go for a short ride this afternoon and start getting to know each other again?"

Well, they went for that short ride and her father did begin to laugh again".

LOVE AND LIES

Anne's expression turned pensive and then she said "I know just how her father felt. *I still miss someone* after all these years, and *I go to pieces* if I dwell on him for too long. *I know a heartache* will take a *hold on me* if I let it; however, I do know that my *broken bleeding hurtin' heart* will disappear when a *brand new love* comes along.

After I had left the *Peppimenatri Cradle* Station area, which is a very large station area, heading for *bluer skies,* I ran into an *old pal of yesterday,* Sally, who used to live on the other side of the *silos of home.* We were such good friends and we did just about everything together.

One day she took me *sailing* on the *Neverland* Lake and that's where I met Paul, who had the cutest smile and the most amazing blue eyes that I had ever seen.

He said to me *"Take my hand."* as I got into the sailing boat that was moored to the jetty.

When it was Sally's turn to get into the boat, that *darlin' pal of mine* made an excuse and took off, running back down the jetty to shore.

Paul commented "That'll be right, *she's going again;* she never comes out on the lake with us, even though she makes all the arrangements. Well, I suppose that we'll see her at *the dance* tonight".

I had a wonderful day with Paul and that evening when we met at the dance, he gave me *one rose* and *out of the blue,* he asked me if I would be his girl. He told me that he had had enough sitting in *a place called lonesome* with *a bottle of wine and Patsy Cline.*

In those *sweet moments, love's old song* began playing again and I thought *"There goes my heart again,* he's done a *hit and run* job on it." Well, he didn't actually run. We were together for just over two years and then I found out by accident, while *waiting for a train,* that *all he did was tell me lies* as I saw him with a *lady with a braid.*

When he came home late that night, he popped the question and I asked him *"Are you wasting my time?"* and I told him about what I had seen earlier that day.

9

He didn't say anything straight away, but I waited for an *uproar* of denial to start, instead he said *"Baby with you* I feel as if I am going *crazy* and *I guess we've been together too long.* If I stay with you much longer, you'll have to *bury me beneath the willow* tree back in *my town* that's *in the heart of the land.* Besides, *your love's not enough* for me anymore and you'll *feel a whole lot better* once I get the train home."

I said to him "That *train leaves here this morning,* get on it and don't *come back again. Don't blame me* for your *homestead blues."*

His *hold on me* was not as strong as I thought it was; however, I still jumped into my *old sunlander van* and headed for my *old Aunt Elisa's* place because I didn't want to stay where I was lonely.

As I went to *drive away* from the stop light, just up the road from where I was living, I saw some strange *lights in the mirror* of the van, but they didn't scare me; in fact, I became quite calm.

It wasn't long after that, that I did something unusual; I stopped to pick up a hitch hiker, who said as he was getting into my van "Hello Anne, thank you for stopping for me."

I looked at him and realized that he was *the Cunnamulla feller, the lame fiddler* that I had occasionally spoken to.

He told me that this would be the *last drive* that I would have in the old van, but I would be *travellin' still...always will* keep travelling away from the *train wreck of emotions* that I was in. Then he said something I didn't understand which was *"If you won't go away,* then you can't *come back again.* The *seed of music* has already been planted in your soul.

Somebody loves you but *take your time* before you accept the *fool's gold ring* for he will always have *anecdotes of you.* I stand in the *ring of fire* and see many *rainbows over your blues."*

Then he asked me to pull over near a clump of trees beside the road, which I did. He got out and walked over to the clump of trees and disappeared and about two minutes after that; I saw the *strange lights in the mirror* again that flew off into the distance.

Then, as I was sitting there trying to comprehend what I has just witnessed, I heard *"When the rain tumbles down in July,* your rainbows will chase your blues away as you *change your name."*

10

I arrived at my aunt's place and told her about what *the lame fiddler* had told me.

Her face became very pale with a *frozen emotion* for a few seconds, before she told me "*Many mothers* have told me of similar stories of such a person, but I never believed them, but the *whites of your eyes* are showing me it's true."

"*Every fool has a rainbow* covering them." said Felicity. "When you *turn out the light,* a *new shadow* appears and a *little cricket* can sometimes be heard making his little sound. *In my dreams,* there are *no mistakes* with that *dear someone* on my *planet of love.*"

Kasey said "Sometimes dreaming can be the *sweetest waste of time* because you can have *all the time in the world* to go places and meet people.

I remember one dream I had, *just like yesterday.* I remember the *colour of a carnival* that was *big in Japan* and the little *monkey on a wire* that did tricks for the banana reward that *the captain* gave it. The *tourist* would clap and cheer until the *monkey on a wire* did another trick for which he was rewarded with some more banana.

Other times I would ride *Rattlin' Bones* out into the *Nullabor, the biggest backyard* that any child could have and my *imagination* would take over. If I felt *a little bit lonesome,* I would become an *invisible girl* who would fly with a *little bird* to the top of a mountain. *This mountain* was special, and I sat on top of it because I told myself that *no one hurts up here* and love will *always be on your side.*

On a bad day, I would fly my *little bird* to *Hollywood,* where I could walk with the *monkey on a wire* until I got the *acrobat ache* in my feet, or I could become a *wayward angel* in a film and after being found *guilty as sin* for flying at the *speed of the sound of* …whatever, I could say heavenly "*My oh my* was I really flying that fast."

Then I had to *bring back my heart* and head because *down here on earth; woe is me* if I was out after dusk. That's the way it was with the *southern kind of life* that we led. Dad; being a real *family man* was strict and brought us up *the hard way;* just like he was and he had a *short fuse* so if you upset him, he would say "*I know what you need.*" and he would find a punishment that he knew you didn't like."

11

"And what punishment was that?" asked Beccy.

"It was usually helping to clean out the stables for a week." said Kasey.

"OOO, *sorry I asked*. That is definitely not *bad news for the blues*." replied Beccy "But you can only be *so good for so long* before trouble comes looking for you or you go looking for trouble.

I remember one afternoon, back in *Blackwood Hill,* some young boys were chasing a *wild turkey* through the bush and because I had the *single girl blues* that day, I joined them and when they started climbing the trees, so did I, but on that day I wasn't wearing my jeans.

It took me a short while to figure out why the boys were letting me climb first and when I did realize, I shouted down to them "*Don't look up my dress.*"

My brother told on me to my dad and I really got into trouble, but even more so when I said "*Can I trade him in* for someone who is not a squealer?" That evening *under the new moon,* I wished that I was in *someone else's shoes* after dad had finished with me.

The following day at church, I think my dobbing brother and I had *opposite prayers* and after the last *hymn* was sung, my brother bolted out of the church, down to the dam and swam out to the *lifeboat.*

Everyone was outside the church talking when some loud noises were heard coming from *across the great divide* between the hills and someone shouted out "*That's the sound* of rifle fire.*"

I don't know why, but I started to run down to the dam and when I got there the lifeboat was *sinking,* it was *goin' gone* to the bottom of the dam. I asked the boys standing around watching where my brother was, but no-one knew. If he was dead, we would never know because his body was never found, nothing, not a trace but I felt in *this heart* that he was still alive and I still feel the same way today.

For a month after that day, I used to go to the dam and *skip a stone* or two across the water and one day, a man I'd never seen before was standing and looking out across the dam and as I approached he turned and looked at me with the most breath taking blue eyes I have ever seen.

12

For some reason I had to *turn to a stranger that I hardly know* to ask
"*How wrong is it to feel this free* and know that I'll never be called *lazy
bones* by my brother again?"

The stranger looked at me with his breath taking blue eyes and said
"*Life goes on* but keep *those memories of you* and your brother close to
your heart and you will become a *better woman* for doing so. You and
your brother did have *opposite prayers* on the day he disappeared but you
will meet him again."

As the man walked away towards *Blackwood Hill,* I thought to myself
"*Sorry I asked.*"

That evening, I told my parents about the man at the dam and mum said
that he was *crazy* and could be dangerous, so I had better stay away from
the dam.

When I went to protest, dad said "Your *mother knows best* so just listen
to her and do as she says."

"I'm glad that I'm not *fifteen again* and living back home." said
Melinda. "*Sgt Bean,* our neighbour, used to tell us that it's the *small stuff*
that you do wrong that will land you *smack dab* in the middle of big
trouble. It's *simple to say* these things to you, but once you get a bad
reputation, *people don't change* their thinking of what you've become, no
matter how much you change in yourself and *living it down* is much
harder; even if you were the *teacher's pet* at school."

When I was little, I had an imaginary friend who was a talking dog and
if someone came to visit and I didn't like them, I used to say "*My dog
don't like you.*" but as I got older, my dad took my imaginary friends
from me and *put 'em in a box* for *safe keeping* and wrote one word three
times on the box, *Perhaps, Perhaps, Perhaps,* which stood for the initials
of my imaginary friends.

A few months after dad did that, I went looking for the box and dad
told me, that the night before, he saw it disappearing into the valley and
he couldn't go after it because it was too dark. He suggested that I call out
to them and if they answered; tell them to come home.

So I went to the valley and called out "*Can you hear me down the
hillside?*"

No answer came back so I knew then, it was time I started growing up."

After a short period of silence between the girls, Tania said "I know I'm the youngest here, and I haven't been away from home for very long but there is one thing that I have noticed, and I thought it was just with my generation and after hearing what you girls have said, has made me think.

Whenever I go out on a date or with friends, most males prefer to gather either around the bar or the tables to drink and talk about lots of things. I admit we girls do the same but if we want to dance, the boys won't get up unless they are nagged to death and that the other males then make fun of the ones who do get up to dance.

When they are all together, they sit or stand there comparing one girl against the other. Again, I admit that we do the same; however, we tend to accept most males for who they are and we stick by them.

Men of all ages, on the other hand, look at the females and if they don't like what they see, they don't have much to do with us. Some females are beautiful on the outside but on the inside, they are a waste of time; but other females are just ordinary on the outside, but on the inside, we are more precious than diamonds.

Many females have made the right choice for their partner and through thick and thin they have stuck together, working through their problems when they arose. Some females think that they have made the right choice but when problems arise, they quit without trying to sort things out and it's usually the guy who bails out first.

Can any of you girls tell me why this is so? Is it just male ego, the way they're brought up or just peer pressure from his mates and society?"

MEN AND WOMEN

The other girls looked at Tania with surprised looks; like they couldn't believe that at such young age, she would think of such a thing.

Then Beccy said "Darling, I don't think that anybody can answer your question, not even the men themselves. Why *men don't dance anymore* depends on them. Some men don't dance because they don't know how to and others know how to, but don't dance.

It's the same for us women but we usually go out there to enjoy ourselves. Some of us know how to dance and others don't and a few of us fake it on the floor.

The majority of men do look at the beautiful females; however, they also look for other qualities in the woman they choose for their partner.

If you were to look at all those beautiful women in twenty years' time after they have had a family, you would find that those who still look as beautiful today as they did before they got married, would spend a lot of time and money to keep themselves looking that way and because of that, other parts of their lives suffer. You only have to look at some movie star's life to see what I mean.

Don't ever try to change to be someone you're not, because you'll never really be happy.

The men are the same, just imagine how a body builder would look in twenty years' time when he can't keep up with his exercise regime, especially if he runs a cattle station and has a few kids.

Some men look at beautiful looking girls, but the attraction of a *natural woman* is where her beauty comes from, within, it's *what matters most*.

My *biggest disappointment* with the society of today is; that push for every female to look like a *poster girl*. I think it would be a *cool world* if all the *girls out here* could start a new *come as you are* trend and then it wouldn't matter how tall you were or what size you were, the world would accept you and the *poster girl* would be going, *goin' gone,* plus it would be one of the *little victories* for us bigger girls."

15

"I agree with you." said Melinda "but you also have to look at your *family tree* and see how past relatives looked and what genes they passed on, and not only the genes, but whatever else they passed on that would *give us a happy home.*

Damn love! It can make us or break us, but the events in our lives, happens in *Gods time* and is *outside* of our control.

I wanna be married and *love the night away* every night with the person of my dreams. I want to be wearing *white jeans* and jacket when he says to me "*I'll take care of you.*" but I'm not wasting *my oxygen* on something that won't happen.

Why won't it happen? Because *I like men in trucks* as they are *real people,* just like the mothers who yell out when the *Spaghetti is ready.*

Then there's the demanding person who demands time by saying "*TV or me,* make your choice?" If they were more *understanding* and less demanding, maybe a choice would not have to be made. No one can answer for anyone else because we can't think or see what the other person or people are thinking.

Everybody loves a lover and one day he'll come along. Take my mum and dad, they've been married for fifty years and *he still calls her angel.*"

"Come on girls, *here we are* running men down and not looking at their good points. *I'm thinking of my blue eyes* right now and he's making me feel happy. He would be a good *sight for sore eyes* if I saw him right now, even though I know I won't. I would give anything for him to *come back again* so I can go *sailing* with him, *safe in the arms of love.*

Only love can break your heart and my love's wearing *long ago shoes.* *Those long ago shoes,* when *all he did was tell me lies* about being home with *a bottle of wine and Patsy Cline.* And yes; I got a *broken bleeding hurtin' heart* from him but that can happen on the *merry-go-round of life.*

Even when *I'm thinking tonight of my blue eyes,* will I remember the sweet love that I had for him. I suppose I'll make *the same mistake* again and end up *heartbroken* by some *grievous angel* but I'll *never say never* to love and the *sweet moments* of it; however, *out of the blue* will come the love that will last forever.

16

Many mothers comfort, support and are there for their children when they're a *train wreck of emotion* and they'll say *"We'll sweep the ashes out in the morning* when you'll *feel a whole lot better."*

Tania, *you can believe in me* when I say that *forever never felt so far away* when I covered my heart with a *long black veil* that I also locked away so no-one could get to it. I have learnt over the years just how to take care of this *careless heart* of mine. *Take your time* to find someone; you're still young, so live your life and enjoy it while you can." said Anne.

"That's right. *Your day will come* and when Mr. Right does come along, your *crazy heart* will have your head flying around like a *little bird."* said Kasey. "One day, *Poppa Bill* says to me that *"If I were you* I should let *the devils inside my head* help me to learn and grow, but not let them take me over. The *devil on your back* has *already gone* and he won't *follow you home* again. *You got the car,* so make good use of it. *The woe is mine,* when your *mother, Adeline* finds out that I have told you that because I know that she would prefer to keep you here at *home,* to keep the *home fires* burning.

We got along very well *before you came along* and we'll get along just as well once you've left home. Well; that's if your mother doesn't have me *sleeping cold* again in the shed. You know she made me do that once when I put this house up *for sale* without discussing it with her first. I learnt my lesson quickly and I swore on the *hard last Bible* that I'd never do it again unless your mother wanted to move." commented Anne and then continued saying *"The best years* of your life are to come, so be *the captain* and allow yourself to become *stronger* every day.

Don't become a *monkey on a wire* that can only go from point A to point B. *Sometimes,* life can be a *hard road* to follow, but if you can find the funny side of most issues, then life doesn't seem so bad.

You would not believe some of *the stupid things I do* to bring myself up when I'm feeling down, but, whatever you do, don't *surrender to another lonely day* or they will keep coming and stay with you until you feel like a *train wreck."*

Beccy stated *"Just because she always has* someone to talk to when she's down, doesn't mean that everyone has someone or is able to talk about what's bothering them.

Usually I find a place where I can go and *just shout* at the world, and the best place for me to go is where the *Galleries of Pink Galahs,* from the carnival was situated at the base of *Blackwood Hill*. Believe me, when I do it; it's *bad news for the blues* and the wild turkey that may be hanging around.

Oh, and Tania, *men don't dance anymore* because they don't want to.

Don't ever say "*Sorry I asked.*" because unless you ask, you never get answers and learn from them. Some may not be the right answer, but unless you ask, you won't know.

Getting back to what we were saying about men, just remember, they say the same or similar things about us. They love us, they hurt us, they leave us but the main thing is, they can't live without us and guess what; we can't live without them either, no matter how hard we try to. That's what makes the world go round."

The girls laughed and unanimously said "You're right you know."

Then Melinda said "I would dearly love to say to someone "*I love you, you're perfect, now change.*"

The girls laughed again before Felicity said "*Now that's what I call love*. A perfect somebody to have around. There again, if he were perfect all the time, he would become quite boring after a while and I'd be the one who would have to be mischievous, just to have some fun with him."

"No." said Beccy "I would like one of the wild ones who would make me laugh and be a bit unpredictable and never whisper "*Say you love me.*" in my ear because he would know that I did love him without him having to ask me."

Kasey said "*This story* makes me laugh now, but at the time it wasn't funny.
One night, during a storm, the family was sitting around talking and I said "Dad, *do you remember* when I was going out with *Hank,* the son of *Georgia Brown* and you had all that trouble with the tractor?

Well, when we were out in the shed that afternoon, we thought that there was *something in the water* container near where the dogs play, so instead of throwing it out, we moved it to the other side of the shed and

18

then after the tractor trouble, we realized that it was *water in the fuel* that you had put on one side so you wouldn't use it."

That night, I wished that I was the *invisible girl,* so that I could duck the *crossfire* of looks and words that was going back and forth. Dad said I did the right thing by moving it so the dogs wouldn't drink it, but he said that I should have told him and he would have disposed of it properly."

"Oh, look, here comes James, so I suppose we should get ready to go with him." said Felicity.

James arrived to where the girls were standing and said "Sorry girls, I'm afraid that there will be a further delay. About another fifteen minutes and we should be ready to start."

He looked straight at Tania giving her a quick smile and then turned and walked back up the *grassy* mound.

THE MYSTERY MAN

"Tania. Tania, you're *standing too close to the fire* so mind you don't get burnt." said Anne.

Tania looked at Anne with an awed look on her face.

"Oh no! Tania; No… No. *As if I didn't know* what that look on your face means. You don't even know who he is, or anything about him." continued Anne.

"Did you girls see his electrifying blue eyes and that fascinating smile of his? He really has the *Twang factor*. I know I don't know him but I would really like to." said Tania.

All the girls looked at each other and then back to Tania and said in unison "The what factor?"

Felicity asked "What does twang mean?"

"Don't you know? Twang means, the wonderful all-round nice guy." said Tania.

"Tania, I saw your face too. You could *light up a candle* with the sparks that came out of your eyes."

The tone of Kasey's voice changed when she continued on saying "You could *sing on the door* of *the house that never was* if you think that you could have him *falling into you* with just one small smile. I doubt that he would be available to spend much time with you, least of all today."

Realizing what she had just said and the way she had said it, Kasey looked at Tania and said "*Don't look so sad,* I didn't mean to upset you; but *the devil's inside my head* again and sometimes I say the meanest things. *The woe is mine* and *someone like me* should know better than to let their tongue runaway like a *runaway train*. I'm sorry. Actually, I think that he could be *the sweetest waste of time* for you right now."

"I think he's cute." said Anne "and he's a beautiful *sight for sore eyes*. I think that you could be *safe in the arms of love* with him. When this shing-dig is over, I'll try and talk to him and see what I can find out about him. OK."

20

"Just think, if nothing comes of this brief encounter, you can always *dream him home* and have a *secret love affair* with him. Wait a minute, *what was I thinking!* If he's available, go for it but be careful of *the L word.*

When he looked and smiled at you, he reminded me of someone I saw in a café called The *3 Rings.* For some reason, I can't remember his name, and I don't usually forget men's names; however, this guy had the most mysterious blue eyes that you could imagine and a smile that would melt the *heart of a woman* of any age. I think he had fair hair and the reason I noticed him, was because he was alone. No-one who looked as good as him, should've been alone, but he left before I was able to speak with him." said Melinda.

"Hhmm." said Kasey "A few years ago, after I had had an argument with my dad over the phone because he told me that "I had *better be home soon* or not come home at all." I was sitting under a tree in the park on the other side of the town we lived in, and the tears were flowing *like a river,* when a *bluebird* flew past me and landed in a patch of trees close by.

A few minutes later, from *somewhere* out of the trees, this really nice looking male came up to me and gave me a *wildflower.* He had really hypnotic blue eyes and the most sensuous smile that *saturated* all my negative feelings with love and peace that made me *bring back my heart* to love again and sent *the devils inside my head* away. Every now and then they return, just like before, but they soon disappear if I think of that blue eyed stranger. Sometimes *I still pray* that I will run into him again because he was *more than ordinary* men are."

Felicity butted in with "Hang on a minute; this is weird. We only met James for the first time about an hour ago, and a few minutes ago, he looked and smiled at Tania, making her eyes light up like the *landing lights* on a plane. Now; each of us, including me, are saying that we have all had an encounter with a man, who for me, had the most astounding blue eyes and the most astonishingly, heart-warming smile. Did this man, that you have all met, seem like he was ageless, like you couldn't really tell how old he was?"

All the girls nodded their heads to say yes.

Felicity continued "I met my guy just after I had booked into a *bed & breakfast* hotel called the *Western Lullaby.*

21

I was desperately trying to get away from Billy, who kept following me from town to town. He used to jump trains to do so, and *that boy sure could jump a train,* even when it was moving.

Well, we had a bit of an argument and I told him that if he saw *less of me more often,* then we would have more to talk about when we did see each other, but he wouldn't listen to me.

He told me "*If you were my baby,* I'd stay with *you till the rivers all run dry.*"

I needed to get away from him; I needed to *breathe* fresh air and have plenty of time to think. Most importantly, I needed my space for a while. So I hired a car and drove out to the hotel.

My blue eyed guy came over to me as I was looking out over the valley from the side porch and said "*The flood* may have taken your mother away, and at the time, taken the joy out of your father's heart, but you put it back again. *Remember you* are a special person to those who truly love you. You will find happiness when making others happy and love will come to you from the strangest place, when you least expect it."

He then kissed me on the forehead and walked away.

I went looking for him to ask how he knew about my mother and father, but he had gone and I've never seen him since.

Seeing James, reminded me of the guy I just spoke about and I am feeling warm, peaceful and calm."

Beccy said "You know I'm feeling the same. I have never told anyone this before, but before my blue eyed guy walked away, he kissed me on the cheek."

"I never spoke to my blue eyed feller." said Melinda. "But he left me a note with the waitress. I have lost the note but I remember the strange message. "*Rest your weary mind* like *there's a bridle hanging on the wall* of your bedroom. *Life's too long to live like this, it's magic* for you will work and when you do find it, *I'll see you in my dreams*." To this day I'm still trying to work out what that message meant. Just talking about it, has me feeling the same way as you girls."

Anne said "The lamer fiddle was a feller from Cunnamulla, but he took me by the hand and kissed it before he walked away from the van and when the strange lights appeared in the mirror of the van, I felt then, as I feel now, just like the rest of you girls, happy, peaceful, warm and calm."

Then Tania said "Are you sure that you saw all these guys, who you each describe like being the same one and now you are saying that James could be every one of them. Could this be just a coincidental meeting of sorts? All of your fellers had the similar things in common that were blue eyes and a gorgeous smile, but no names."

James startled Tania when he walked up behind her and said "Tania, will you come with me for a minute please, I need to talk to you."

James walked Tania to a rose garden that was a short distance from where the other women were standing, but out of hearing distance from them.

James said "*A farmer's prayer* is *an Irish blessing* to some people. Don't ever think that *life don't get much better than this. Getting' a grip* on life and *livin' the dream* that you have, will be better the *second time around.*"

He kissed her on the cheek and as he walked away he said "We'll meet again. I always know where to find you. I like the way that you think that I have the twang factor."

Tania walked back to the girls in a daze and said "How long had he been standing behind me?"

"We were just discussing that very question; nobody even saw him there until he spoke. One of us would have seen him if he had been standing there a while. What did he say to you?" said Felicity.

When Tania repeated what he had said, Anne asked "Does any of that make any sense to you?"

"Not really, but what did he mean when he said that he always knows where to find me? Do you think that I'll have to worry about my safety now?" said Tania.

Felicity said "We all saw him kiss you on the cheek, so how are you feeling now?"

"Strangely, I feel warm, peaceful, happy and calm; all rolled into one and I feel safe. So, could he be all our blue eyed guys but coming to us in different disguises?" said Tania.

The girls looked at each other as if one of them would know the answer to Tania's question and Beccy started to laugh while trying to say "Men are right about us women when they say that we can't make up our minds, it's true you know. Here we are, one minute complaining and bitching about men and why *men don't dance anymore* and the next minute, we're all talking about some guy we've met, who is the complete opposite to what we've just said.

If I should ever bump into my blue eyed guy again, I wouldn't say much to him, but I would be thinking "*Kiss me where I stand* and *say you love me* so I can keep *those memories of you* and those great feelings locked inside me forever. I would always have something good to think of and to make me happy when things are tough for me."

"Back in *my town, in the country,* some of the townsfolk say "*Mammas don't let your babies grow up to be cowboys*." if a boy is born or if it's a girl, they say, "Don't let them grow up to be a *honky tonk girl*." because the child may never leave home and see what life is like in other places in this world.

I had enough of *cryin' time* and hearing the *honky tonk blues,* so I said *goodbye* to the place, caught the *eastbound train* out of there and *I don't go back anymore,* that's why I'm *travellin' still, always will.* Maybe one day, I'll meet my blue eyes again." said Anne.

"I always thought that I was *not pretty enough,* so I wanted to become the invisible girl." said Kasey. "Then one day after meeting my blue eyes, I said to myself "*I can change* and become *the captain* of my life. *The woe is mine* if I don't do it." I did do it, and for a while; I was *living in the circle* where the little girl in me was *lost & found* the woman in me; however, I wasn't really happy until I found the balance between them both.

Even as a woman, I found that I still needed the little girl in me at times. I can be myself now and it doesn't matter if I am with the *millionaires* or the people who have practically *nothing at all*."

24

"*The letting go* of your childhood and saying *goodbye house,* the only place that you really knew and felt safe in, for me, was hard especially *when the last child leaves home* and I happened to be the last child to leave home.

I'm *awake now* to the way that God moves in his mysterious ways and now with him *watching over me,* I feel as *if love's out to get me* and this time; it will be a *truly true love* that will always last." said Melinda.

Beccy looked at the faces of the other girls and said "*How wrong it is,* for anyone to think that they can make it on their own without any help.

You could be sitting *under the new moon* with the *single girl blues* and feeling so down, that you look to the sky and ask "God, *do I ever cross your mind?"*

But you know in your heart that you do cross his mind so you look up again and say "*Sorry I asked* because if I didn't cross your mind, I wouldn't be *strong enough to bend* and *too strong to break* at life's little curve balls that are sent my way. *Mother knows best* when she tells you to keep the faith because *life goes on* no matter what you do."

SECOND CHANCES

Felicity said "*My life* back in *Swingtown* was pretty ordinary. Most of the guys were into some kind of automotives, whether it be *two wheels* or four. I did have a steady boyfriend, but did *I fall* in love with him? Not really.

One day we had an argument over something trivial and he said that he was leaving, so I said to him "*So go on, you can't break my heart.*" and he left. A few weeks later, he rang me and wanted to *take me back,* but I told him to forget it.

I was quite happy being on my own, besides I could make *no mistakes* that would get me into trouble. I had my girlfriends to go out with and my grades at school landed me in a very good, well paid, promotions job, which allowed me to travel constantly. I met Billy on one of my trips and that's also when I met my blue eyes."

"Don't worry Felicity, *your day will come* and then you and that special someone will make *love like a hurricane.* You have to *hold on* and believe that there is that special person for you *down here on earth.*"

I got into a *beautiful mess* with someone who had a *short fuse* and I got out and away from it. *I still pray* for that special someone.

A friend said once "*I wish it would rain men,* so I could choose the one for you; however, being with someone is different from being with the right one.

I told her "I am *the captain* of my life, so don't go thinking that *if I needed you* to *set me up* with someone, I would like the person you chose. *That's what makes a broken friendship* if things go wrong." said Kasey.

"Well, if it did rain men and I got the wrong one, *can I trade him in* for another one?" said Beccy.

All the girls burst out laughing over Beccy's comment.

Anne looked at her watch and said "If they keep us hanging around much longer, you will have to *bury me beneath the willow* tree over there and every year, you'll all have to *come back again* and *cry like a man* over me."

The girls laughed again.

Then Anne carried on saying "You can have the *one day blues* and pretend that you are a *darling pal of mine*. At least you would be better than Paul; because *all he did was tell me lies* and you'll remember me because *that's all you ever got from me,* a good laugh *with inserts from* each and every one of you."

Beccy said "Laughter is *bad news for the blues* and *those memories of you* that we will have is what matters most. We can always say that we put you to *rest in pieces under the new moon.*

If you girls are still around, which I hope you are, when I get old, *just shoot me* and have a *come as you are* party afterwards but please don't do the *Bushland Boogie* 'cos I hate that dance, just *keep on rockin'*. If the *men don't dance;* then tell them to find a river where they can *skip a stone* over it and then go and bring the same stone back."

Kasey said "If we ever had to shoot you, then I'll bring *the flower. We're all gonna die some day* but I doubt that it will be anytime in the near future.

"*Am I the only one* getting tired of waiting? Why hasn't James come with an update of what's going on?" Anne asked the other girls and then she said "Hang on, *I spy* someone coming now, but it isn't James."

The girls turned to see a more matured gentleman approaching them.

As he stopped in front of them, he said "Good, you girls have arrived, so now we can get started."

He looked at Anne and continued saying "Now Lisa, would you please introduce me to your sisters?"

Anne said "*I'm not Lisa* and these women are not my sisters. Who are you and where is James? We have been standing here for nearly an hour and really, I don't know why I am here? I received a hand delivered note telling me to meet these other girls here today, but it never said what for."

Then each of the other girls said "So did I. I got a hand delivered note saying the same thing. Maybe James can explain what's going on?"

The man said "My name is Gary and who is this James person that you've been talking to and if you're not Lisa and these women are not your sisters, then who are all of you?"

Anne said "My name is Anne and these other girls are Kasey, Beccy, Felicity, Melinda and…"

Tania butted in and said "I'm Tania and James is the nice blonde haired guy with the beautiful blue eyes and the terrific smile."

Gary's face went pale and then he asked "Have any of you girls seen James before today?"

"Yes." said the girls

"Except for Tania, she only met him today." said Felicity.

Gary took a deep breath and said "Oh my goodness. It can't be who I'm thinking of. Would you girls answer these questions for me please? When you girls met this James before, did he give a name and was it just after a traumatic or upsetting event?"

The girls gave the same answer "No, he didn't give them a name and yes, it was after an upsetting event."

Gary's face turned even paler as he said "I believe that all you girls have had an encounter with someone known as Earth Angel David. He appears every so often to help people through difficult times. He gives them a special kind of love, hope and a message. You may never understand the message at the times he gives it to you, but as your life progresses, so do the messages begin to make sense. You are all very lucky to be touched by him."

"Are you making fun of us; because if you are, then I for one am not amused. We have all rearranged our day but we don't know what for, plus, we have been standing here for an hour now. So please tell us exactly who we are here for?" said Felicity.

"Well." said Gary "Firstly, I am deadly serious about David and I'm not making fun of you. Secondly, we are here to lay Tyrone to rest."

28

"Tyrone! Tyrone who?" said Kasey.

"Not Tyrone who." said Gary "Tyrone the pink galah. He is *Annie Johnson*'s bird. He supposedly told Annie to "*Bury me beneath the willow* tree when I die so I can go to the *Galleries of Pink Galahs* and lay in peace there.""

Kasey said "I thought I was here for the funeral of *Mr. Baylis,* our old next door neighbour."

Anne said "I thought I was here for the funeral of *Hayes,* my aunt's husband."

Beccy said "I thought I was here for the funeral of *Jesse,* a girlfriend's sister, who's been ill for a long time."

Melinda said "I thought I was here for the funeral of *Rapunzel,* an old school friend's father, who came here to live from overseas."

Felicity said "I thought I was here for the funeral of my wonderful old school principle, *Mr. Catfish.*"

"Well." said Tania "If you all thought you came here for the funeral of someone else, who am I here for, or rather, why am I here?"

Gary looked a bit surprised and puzzled and said "You were all meant to meet each other today. I don't know why, but by all accounts, *that was the plan* that David or James had in mind for you all. You are welcome to join us in singing Tyrone's favourite song *The Ballad Of Poppa Bill.*"

Then Kasey said "If *you make me sing,* then you had better get the other girls to sing as well. I have no idea what we would sound like, singing all together."

Anne said "Sorry, but I think I'll go and find somewhere to get a drink and something to eat. Do you girls want to join me?"

The other girls declined Gary's offer and decided to go with Anne.

Anne said "I have *wheels* parked outside the gate. Let's go to the *Showman's Daughter* Club in *Sin City* and it's not a *Honky Tonk* place either. I've heard that the *Grievous Angel* band has a new guitarist and they're playing at the club tonight.

Today has been messed up for me, so tonight *I'll shoot the moon* while *I'm thinking tonight of my blue eyes*."

"You know you're right there, Anne. *Once in awhile,* it's good to get away from things and go *somewhere* different.

One day Tania, you're going to be telling *this story* to your grandchildren and they will think that you've made it up. But I know for as long as you live, you will never forget James with his blue eyes and his smile. *That's more about love* that he gave you than you will get from someone else. *Your day will come,* I promise you that." said Kasey.

Melinda looked at Tania and said "*She's still got it.* Look at her eyes, they're still sparking. *Love lifted me* up when I needed it, but *you are something else. Some girls* would go crazy if he would *send them love,* like he gave you.

If you're *still here* in this part of Australia in six months' time, then look me up and we'll do something together. You all know that *you got me* as a friend for life."

"I know that when I *come back again* to this town, I'll certainly give you a call and maybe we can have a drink together, maybe at the *Sweet Rain* Bar in *Goulburn Street* and we'll probably cause such an *uproar* with our stories that *many mothers* will wish their children could have the experience that we've just had." said Anne.

The girls spent the afternoon together and decided to go to the club that night.

As the girls got to the front door of the club, Melinda looked at Beccy, who had stopped walking and said "*What's up?*"

Beccy said "I know the guitar player of the band; that's Danny. *That's the sound* I remember, when Danny made his guitar talk all those years ago at the carnival.

I can't go in there; anyway *this shirt* is not really suitable for the club. I'll go back to the motel and change and *come on in* later this evening."

Beccy heard a voice saying "You're a *better woman,* than Danny has ever met. *It's only the beginning* of a new way of life for him.

This time, under the new moon, you'll see that he's changed. You stood up to him and he learnt his lesson from that and he has never forgotten you."

Beccy turned around to see David disappearing into the crowd going into the club.

Then she saw Danny coming out on his break and thought "*Here you come again.* What do I say to you? What answer should I give if you ask "*Do I ever cross your mind?*" or "*What's up?*" Maybe he won't see me, so what am I worried about. I am in control of my life and he can't do anything about it.

If he starts getting nasty like he did before, all I have to do is walk away. If he has changed like David said he has, then maybe, just maybe, I'll spend some time with him to try to get to know him better."

Kasey looked around to see David in the distance, smiling at her and she heard him say "*I got you now,* but I know that you're *still feeling blue. Your day will come* very soon and *the lost music blues* will go when *the rain* in your heart has gone. *Everybody loves you now,* so that will bring back the *blue skies* for you and the person who will capture your heart will be the *sweetest waste of time* that you will have for the rest of your life."

"Did you see him?" Kasey asked Tania, who was standing beside her.

"Who?" said Tania.

"David." said Kasey "*Am I the only one* who just saw him standing over there?"

Then *out of the blue,* Paul walked up to Anne and handed her *one rose* and said "I have been having *anecdotes of you* since you left and *I'm still coming down from you.* The *train leaves here this morning* or rather tomorrow morning and if you want me to be on it, I'll go now, but I would like to stay and try to work things out.

Only love can break a heart and you broke mine the day you left. I know what I did was wrong and *I got you* to thank for making me see that the *game of love* can really only be played with two people on the *merry-go-round of life.*

31

I know a heartache because I have one; but the only time I really felt *safe in the arms of love* was, *baby with you. You can believe in me* when I say that I'm very sorry and that I'll never hurt you again; if you would just give me another chance and *take me home.*"

Anne glimpsed David over Paul's shoulder, smiling and his blue eyes glowing as she thought "*Hold on me, oh, there goes my heart again.*"

Paul turned to walk away and Anne said "*You ain't going nowhere* yet. *Am I the one* you really want? You know that I'm not *born for the night life* and my job keeps me *travellin' still, always will* until I can get a promotion that will allow me to settle down. My heart's in an *uproar* too, because *I'm still coming down from you.* This time, we'll go slow and get to know each other again and see if our love will grow."

Anne looked back over Paul's shoulder, but David was gone.

Anne asked Paul inquisitively "Did you receive a hand written note telling you to be here at this time today, by any chance?"

Paul looked at Anne with an astonished look on his face and said "Yes, I did; but that's all it had on it. I had no idea that you would be here. Something happened to me a few months after you left. I realized what I had done and who I really wanted to spend the rest of my life with. I stopped seeing a lot of my old friends and I have settled into a decent job. Why did you ask me that?"

"Oh, I was just wondering, that's all." said Anne.

Everyone was introduced to each other and then they all went into the club.

Danny went back on stage with the band and really made his guitar talk for Beccy.

Paul actually got up and had a dance with Anne, who found out that he was really a good dancer.

Beccy bought a round of drinks to the table and Felicity started laughing and said "*Now this is life.*"

32

Tania raised her glass and said "No matter what happens, *she'll be right. Here's to us.*" And then she let out one enormously loud "*Yee Ha.*" that made everybody laugh.

As for David; well, you never know where he'll turn up next or who he will help.

It could be you.

REFERENCES

<u>KASEY CHAMBERS</u>
CARNIVAL CD
COLOUR OF A CARNIVAL
SING ON THE DOOR
THE RAIN
LIGHT UP A CANDLE
HARD ROAD
NOTHING AT ALL
LIVING ON THE RAILROAD
I GOT YOU NOW
SURRENDER
DANGEROUS
YOU MAKE ME SING
DON'T LOOK SO SAD

FAITH & SCIENCE
SAFE AND SOUND
EVERYBODY LOVES YOU NOW
STOLEN CAR
SET ME UP
I KNOW WHAT YOU NEED
ALL THE TIME IN THE WORLD
I CAN CHANGE
ALWAYS BE ON YOUR SIDE
ACROBAT ACHE
BIG IN JAPAN
TOURIST (STAND IN ONE PLACE)
HOME

THE CAPTAIN BONUS DISK
I STILL PRAY
DAM
FREIGHT TRAIN
WATER IN THE FUEL
ANOTHER LONELY DAY
BETTER BE HOME SOON
HEARTBREAK HEARTMEND

BARRICADES & BRICKWALLS CD
BARRICADES & BRICKWALLS
NOT PRETTY ENOUGH
ON A BAD DAY
RUNAWAY TRAIN
A LITTLE BIT LONESOME
NULLABOR SONG
MILLION TEARS
STILL FEELING BLUE
THIS MOUNTAIN
CROSSFIRE
FALLING INTO YOU
IF I WERE YOU
I STILL PRAY

THE CAPTAIN CD
CRY LIKE A BABY
THE CAPTAIN
THE FLOWER
YOU GOT THE CAR
THESE PINES
DON'T TALK BACK
SOUTHERN KIND OF LIFE
MR BAYLIS
THE HARD WAY
HARD LAST BIBLE
DON'T GO
WE'RE ALL GONNA DIE SOME DAY

DEAD RINGER BAND – THE VERY BEST – SO FAR
LIVING IN THE CIRCLE
HOME FIRES
THAT'S WHAT MAKES A BROKEN…
AUSTRALIAN SON
I WISH IT WOULD RAIN
HALF WAY TO SYDNEY
SADDLE BOY
ALREADY GONE
CRAZY HEART
GYPSY BOUND
FAMILY MAN
SPEED OF THE SOUND OF…

AM I THE ONLY ONE (WHO'S EVER FELT THIS WAY)
HE STILL THINKS I CARE
THAT'S MORE ABOUT LOVE
IF I NEEDED YOU
ROAD TO NOWHERE
JUST LIKE YESTERDAY (SONG FOR GRAM)

WAYWARD ANGEL CD
PONY
HOLLYWOOD
STRONGER
BLUEBIRD
MORE THAN ORDINARY
WAYWARD ANGEL
PAPER AEROPLANE
LIKE A RIVER
FOR SALE
FOLLOW YOU HOME
MOTHER
GUILTY AS SIN
LOST & FOUND
SATURATED

RATTLIN BONES CD
RATTLIN BONES
ONCE IN A WHILE
SWEETEST WASTE OF TIME
MONKEY ON A WIRE
ONE MORE YEAR
THE HOUSE THAT NEVER WAS
WILDFLOWER
ON ONE HURTS UP HERE
THE DEVIL'S INSIDE MY HEAD
SLEEPING COLD
ADELINE
JACKSON HOLE
YOUR DAY WILL COME
WOE IS ME

KASEY CHAMBERS, POPPA BILL AND THE LITTLE HILLBILLIES CD BOOKLET (PLASTIC CASE)
THE LOST MUSIC BLUES
THE BALLAD OF POPPA BILL
I SPY
POPPA BILL SAYS
DAD, DO YOU REMEMBER?
BEFORE YOU CAME ALONG
TWO HOUSES
OLD MAN DOWN ON THE FARM
MY OH MY
WHEN WE WERE KIDS
SOMETIMES
SOMETHING IN THE WATER
IMAGINATION
BLUE
CHRISTMAS TIME
THE BEST YEARS

LITTLE BIRD – ALBUM (AUTOGRAPHED)
SOMEONE LIKE ME
BEAUTIFUL MESS
DEVIL ON YOUR BACK
LITTLE BIRD
GEORGIA BROWN
SOMEWHERE
THIS STORY
LOVE LIKE A HURRICANE
DOWN HERE ON EARTH
NULLARBOR (THE BIGGEST BACKYARD)
BRING BACK MY HEART
INVISIBLE GIRL
TRAIN WRECK
THE STUPID THINGS I DO... (HIDDEN TRACK)

LITTLE BIRD (DELUXE VERSION AUTOGRAPHED)
DISC ONE
SOMEONE LIKE ME
BEAUTIFUL MESS
DEVIL ON YOUR BACK
LITTLE BIRD
GEORGIA BROWN

37

SOMEWHERE
THIS STORY
LOVE LIKE A HURRICANE
DOWN HERE ON EARTH
NULLARBOR (THE BIGGEST BACKYARD)
BRING BACK MY HEART
INVISIBLE GIRL
TRAIN WRECK
DISC TWO
MILLIONAIRES
OLD SCHOOL
HOLD ON
KASEY CHAMBERS TALKS ABOUT "LITTLE BIRD" (NOT USED
IN STORY)
DISC THREE – DVD
THE MAKING OF 'LITTLE BIRD' (NOT USED IN STORY)
VIDEO CLIP – 'LITTLE BIRD'

**DVD – RATTLIN BONES THE MAX SESSION INCLUDES 10
SONGS RECORDED LIVE AT THE SYDNEY OPERA HOUSE
PLUSEXCLUSIVE
INTERVIEW WITH KASEY AND SHANE RATTLIN BONES &
MONKEY ON A WIRE**
RATTLIN' BONES
MONKEY ON A WIRE
SWEETEST WASTE OF TIME
THE DEVIL'S INSIDE MY HEAD
YOUR DAY WILL COME
WILDFLOWER
JACKSON HOLE
SHORT FUSE (PART 4)
THE CAPTAIN
WOE IS MINE
KASEY & SHANE INTERVIEW - EXTRA FEATURE (NOT USED IN
STORY)
VIDEO - RATTLIN' BONES - EXTRA FEATURE
VIDEO - MONKEY ON A WIRE - EXTRA FEATURE

**KASEY CHAMBERS & SHANE NICHOLSON LIVE AT THE
SYDNEY OPERA HOUSE – THE MAX SESSIONS CD/DVD**
DISC 1
RATTLIN' BONES - LIVE
MONKEY ON A WIRE - LIVE
THE SWEETEST WASTE OF TIME - LIVE
THE DEVIL'S INSIDE MY HEAD - LIVE
YOUR DAY WILL COME - LIVE
WILDFLOWER - LIVE
JACKSON HOLE - LIVE
SHORT FUSE - LIVE
THE CAPTAIN - LIVE
WOE IS MINE - LIVE
DISC 2
RATTLIN' BONES
MONKEY ON A WIRE - VIDEO
THE SWEETEST WASTE OF TIME - VIDEO
THE DEVIL'S INSIDE MY HEAD - VIDEO
YOUR DAY WILL COME - VIDEO
WILDFLOWER - VIDEO
JACKSON HOLE - VIDEO
SHORT FUSE - VIDEO
THE CAPTAIN - VIDEO
WOE IS MINE
INTERVIEW (NOT USED IN STORY)
RATTLIN' BONES - FILMCLIP
MONKEY ON A WIRE – FILMCLIP

<u>MELINDA SCHNEIDER</u>
BE YOURSELF
BE YOURSELF LYRICS
COURAGEOUS LYRICS
CRY A LITTLE LYRICS
GRASSY LYRICS
I'LL TAKE CARE OF YOU LYRICS
SAFE LYRICS
PEOPLE DON'T CHANGE LYRICS
STILL HERE LYRICS
OUTSIDE LYRICS
BAD DAY LYRICS
UNDERSTANDING LYRICS
THANK YOU LYRICS

AWAKE NOW LYRICS

STRONGER
BIG WORLD SMALL WORLD LYRICS
THAT WAS THE PLAN LYRICS
STRONGER LYRICS
SEND THEM LOVE LYRICS
TRULY TRUE LOVE LYRICS
IN YOUR HEAD LYRICS
THE LETTING GO LYRICS
REST YOUR WEARY MIND LYRICS
I LIKE MEN IN TRUCKS LYRICS
YOU ARE SOMETHING ELSE LYRICS
FIFTEEN AGAIN LYRICS
YOU GOT ME LYRICS
SOMETIMES IT TAKES BALLS TO BE A WOMAN LYRICS

FAMILY TREE
FAMILY TREE LYRICS
SGT. BEAN LYRICS
BEAUTIFUL THING LYRICS
DREAM HIM HOME LYRICS
THE HEALING POWER OF HELPLESS LAUGHTER LYRICS
I WANNA BE MARRIED LYRICS
REAL PEOPLE LYRICS
GOODBYE HOUSE LYRICS
THE L WORD LYRICS
WHAT WAS I THINKING LYRICS
SPAGHETTI IS READY LYRICS

THE KITCHEN TABLETAPES
THERE'S A BRIDLE HANGING ON THE WALL LYRICS
MY DOG DON'T LIKE YOU LYRICS
WHEN THE LAST CHILD LEAVES HOME LYRICS
I'M MY OWN GRANDPA LYRICS
LOVE LIFTED ME LYRICS

HAPPY TEARS
THE STORY OF MY LIFE LYRICS
DAMN LOVE LYRICS
LIVING IT DOWN LYRICS
HE STILL CALLS HER ANGEL LYRICS

SUPERWOMAN LYRICS
CAN YOU HEAR ME DOWN THE HILLSIDE LYRICS
WHEN THE LAST CHILD LEAVES HOME LYRICS
GODS TIME LYRICS
SMALL STUFF LYRICS
I LOVE YOU, YOU'RE PERFECT, NOW CHANGE LYRICS
SHE'S STILL GOT IT LYRICS
NO MORE TEARS TO CRY LYRICS
WEARING WHITE LYRICS

MY OXYGEN
TV OR ME LYRICS
LOOK ME UP LYRICS
SIMPLE TO SAY LYRICS
FROM THE INSIDE OUT LYRICS
COUNT TO 3 LYRICS
3 RINGS LYRICS
MY OXYGEN LYRICS
LIFE'S TOO LONG TO LIVE LIKE THIS LYRICS
RAPUNZEL LYRICS
GIVE US A HAPPY HOME LYRICS
SMACK DAB LYRICS
SOME GIRLS LYRICS
HEART OF A WOMAN LYRICS
WATCHING OVER ME LYRICS
LOVE'S OUT TO GET ME LYRICS
LOVE AWAY THE NIGHT LYRICS
(HEY YOU) COUNT TO THREE LYRICS

**MELINDA SCHNEIDER MELINDA DOES DORIS – A TRIBUTE
TO DORIS DAY**
EVERYBODY LOVES A LOVER
PERHAPS PERHAPS PERHAPS
QUE SERA SERA (WHATEVER WILL BE WILL BE)
IT'S MAGIC
PUT 'EM IN A BOX
BLACK HILLS OF DAKOTA
SECRET LOVE, 8 LOVE SOMEBODY (WITH DAVID CAMPBELL)
THE DEADWOOD STAGE
SENTIMENTAL JOURNEY
TEACHERS PET
I'LL SEE YOU IN MY DREAMS

BECCY COLE
LITTLE VICTORIES CD
BLACKWOOD HILL
LITTLE VICTORIES
LIFE GOES ON
UNDER THE NEW MOON
SORRY I ASKED
THAT'S THE SOUND
SINGLE GIRL BLUES
THIS TIME
JUST SHOUT
BIG BROTHER
MEN DON'T DANCE ANYMORE
WHAT MATTERS MOST
HOW WRONG IT IS
WILD TURKEY

WILD AT HEART / LITTLE VICTORIES CD
THIS HEART
TOO STRONG TO BREAK
WILD AT HEART
NEVER SEES ANYTHING THROUGH
KEEP ON ROCKIN'
ORDINARY WORLD
STORM IN A D CUP
FRIENDS FOR A LIFETIME (SONG FOR KEGAN)
MOTHER KNOWS BEST - BECCY COLE
EMILY
LAZY BONES
DO I EVER CROSS YOUR MIND [LIVE] - DARREN COGGAN,
BECCY COLE, FELICITY,
BLACKWOOD HILL
LITTLE VICTORIES
LIFE GOES ON
UNDER THE NEW MOON
SORRY I ASKED
THAT'S THE SOUND
SINGLE GIRL BLUES
THIS TIME
JUST SHOOT ME
BIG BROTHER
MEN DON'T DANCE ANYMORE

42

WHAT MATTERS MOST
HOW WRONG IS IT - BECCY COLE, ADAM MILLER
WILD TURKEY

PRELOVED CD
HERE YOU COME AGAIN
INSENSITIVE
DANNY'S SONG
IT'S ONLY THE BEGINNING
YOU WEREN'T IN LOVE WITH ME
THIS SHIRT
YOU AIN'T WOMAN ENOUGH
SECRET LOVE
ONLY LOVE CAN BREAK A HEART
ACROSS THE GREAT DIVIDE
YOU'RE SO SQUARE
BIGGEST DISAPPOINTMENT

FEEL THIS FREE CD
RAINBOWS, DREAMS AND BUTTERFLIES
A BETTER WOMAN
JUST BECAUSE SHE ALWAYS HAS
SO GOOD FOR SO LONG
TO FEEL THIS FREE
CAN'T HAVE THAT
THE CLOWN SONG
LEAVE LOVE OUT OF THIS
HIS HOMETOWN
JESSE
SOME LESSONS
SOMEONE ELSE'S SHOES
GIRLS OUT HERE

JUST A GIRL SINGER (DVD)
KANSAS CITY
COME ON IN (AND MAKE YOURSELF AT HOME)
TURN TO A STRANGER THAT I HARDLY KNOW
SWEET NOTHINGS
DO I EVER CROSS YOUR MIND
CRAZY
HYMN
UNDER THE NEW MOON

43

GUITARS, CADILLACS
BUSHLAND BOOGIE
FOOLIN' AROUND
COW COW BOOGIE
BIG GIRLS
BAD NEWS FOR THE BLUES
BY A FIRE OF GIDGEE COALS
BAD NEWS FOR THE BLUES
SKIP A STONE
LAZY BONES
THIS HEART
KEEP ON ROCKIN'
TOO STRONG TO BREAK
HOW WRONG IS IT
LIFE GOES ON
MOTHER KNOWS BEST
DUELLING BANJOS
THAT'S THE SOUND
WHAT MATTERS MOST
BLACKWOOD HILL
LITTLE VICTORIES
UNDER THE NEW MOON
SINGLE GIRL BLUES
SORRY I ASKED
SOMEONE ELSE'S SHOES
MEN DON'T DANCE ANYMORE
SINGLE GIRL BLUES
WILD TURKEY
THIS HEART
MEN DON'T DANCE ANYMORE
UNDER THE NEW MOON
DON'T LOOK UP MY DRESS
THE TENNESSEE WALTZ
SORRY I ASKED

LIVE @ LIZOTTES
DISC ONE
MEN DON'T DANCE
BETTER WOMAN
BLACKWOOD HILL
LIFEBOAT
SORRY I ASKED

44

GIRLS OUT HERE
OPPOSITE PRAYERS
THOSE MEMORIES OF YOU (FEATURING KASEY CHAMBERS)
NATURAL WOMAN
LAZY BONES
GALLERIES OF PINK GALAHS (FEATURING GINA JEFFREYS &
SARA STORER)
WHAT'S UP
SAY YOU LOVE ME
POSTER GIRL
DISC TWO
KISS ME WHERE I STAND
REST IN PIECES
STRONG ENOUGH TO BEND
WILD ONES
BIG GIRLS
SKIP A STONE
GUITAR TALK
GOIN' GONE
BAD NEWS FOR THE BLUES
CAN I TRADE HIM IN
COOL WORLD
COME AS YOU ARE

2007   LIVE AT LIZZOTTE'S
NATURAL WOMAN
LAZY BONES
GALLERIES OF PINK GALAHS
WHAT'S UP
SAY YOU LOVE ME
POSTER GIRL (WRONG SIDE OF THE WORLD)
MEN DON'T DANCE
BETTER WOMAN
BLACKWOOD HILL
LIFEBOAT
SORRY I ASKED
GIRLS OUT HERE
OPPOSITE PRAYERS
THOSE MEMORIES OF YOU
BONUS DVD
LIFEBOAT
THOSE MEMORIES OF YOU

45

GALLERIES OF PINK GALAHS
WHAT'S UP
POSTER GIRL
SAY YOU LOVE ME
STRONG ENOUGH TO BEND

1997 BECCY COLE
GUITAR TALK
GOIN' GONE
BAD NEWS FOR THE BLUES
CAN I TRADE HIM IN
COOL WORLD
COME AS YOU ARE
KISS ME WHERE I STAND
REST IN PIECES
STRONG ENOUGH TO BEND
WILD ONES
BIG GIRLS
SKIP A STONE

<u>FELICITY URQUHART</u>
MY LIFE ALBUM
FLOOD, THE
ON & ON
BIG BLACK CLOUD
BREATHE
NO MISTAKES
A LITTLE JOY
MY LIFE
LONELY GIRL
THAT BOY SURE CAN JUMP A TRAIN
MR CATFISH
STILL ALIVE
TAKE ME BACK
TURN OUT THE LIGHT

BIG BLACK CLOUD VIDEO
SUGAR TOWN
COUNTRY GIRL
WE'LL NEVER GET ALONG
PLANET OF LOVE
REMEMBER YOU

DEAR SOMEONE
THE FLOOD
MY LIFE
BIG BLACK CLOUD
NO MISTAKES

TURN OUT THE LIGHT
TURN OUT THE LIGHT
JEALOUSY
DEAR SOMEONE (DUET WITH GLEN HANNAH)
TILL THE RIVERS ALL RUN DRY
THAT'S WHAT I CALL LOVE
IF YOU WERE MY BABY (DUET WITH RICK PRICE)

NEW SHADOW
YOU CAN'T BREAK MY HEART
NEW SHADOW
SWINGTOWN
I REMEMBER YOU
PLANET OF LOVE
LIVE A LITTLE
WESTERN LULLABY
LESS OF ME MORE OFTEN
TOO MANY SECRETS
IN MY DREAMS
EVERY FOOL HAS A RAINBOW
THIS IS LIFE

LANDING LIGHTS CD
LITTLE CRICKET
SO GO ON
TWO WHEELS
ALL GOOD FUN
I FALL
GIRL IN THE MALL
OLD MAN TROUBLE
TIME FOR CHANGE
ROLLER COASTER
BED & BREAKFAST
ERNIE'S DAUGHTER
LANDING LIGHTS

TANIA KERNAGHAN
LIVIN' THE DREAM
DAD'S NOT GONNA LIKE IT
SECOND TIME AROUND
TWINKLE IN MY EYE
RIDE OF OUR LIFE
LITTLE PIECE OF PARADISE
THE LAST GREAT ROMANTIC
WE'RE A LOT LIKE EACH OTHER (DUET WITH RAY
KERNAGHAN)
DROVING CATTLE WITH THE BOYS
DON'T FENCE ME IN
FISHIN' IN THE DARK
LIVIN' THE DREAM
AN IRISH BLESSING

BIG SKY COUNTRY
GOIN' BUSH
HEART OF A MAN
LASSOO YOU
STEAL AWAY
DROVERS BOY
FARMER'S PARAYER
SHE'LL BE RIGHT
THE MONGREL
TOO LITTLE LOVE
GETTIN' A GRIP
BOOTS N' ALL
BIG SKY COUNTRY

HIGHER GROUND CD
YEE HA!
30 SOMETHING
HARLEY MCTAGGART
HERE'S TO US
PRICE YOU PAY
TWANG FACTOR
PICKING UP THE PIECES
RIDE WITH ME BAREBACK
I WILL
LIFE DON'T GET MUCH BETTER THAN THIS
HIGHER GROUND

ANNE KIRKPATRICK
ANNE KIRKPATRICK & FRIENDS LIVE
OUT OF THE BLUE
YOU AIN'T GOIN' NOWHERE (WITH TROY CASSAR-DALEY)
ONE ROSE
I STILL MISS SOMEONE (WITH JANE SAUNDERS)
SIN CITY (WITH IAN SIMPSON & JAMES GILLARD)
WHEELS (WITH DAVID KIRKPATRICK AND THE TRAVELLING
COUNTRY BAND)
FEEL A WHOLE LOT BETTER
LIGHTS IN THE MIRROR (WITH GENNI KANE)
CRYIN' TIME (WITH LEE KERNAGHAN)
COME BACK AGAIN (WITH LEE KERNAGHAN)
IF YOU WON'T GO AWAY (WITH THE FLYING EMUS)
IN THE COUNTRY
BURY ME BENEATH THE WILLOW (WITH JOY MCKEAN AND
SLIM DUSTY)

ANNIE'S SONGS
SAILING
GRIEVOUS ANGEL
ANNIE JOHNSON
ALL HE DID WAS TELL ME LIES
LOUISE
JOHN HARDY
FEEL A WHOLE LOT BETTER
I GO TO PIECES
I KNOW A HEARTACHE
UPROAR
HOLD ON ME
OLD AUNT ELISA
CRAZY
I'M THINKING TONIGHT OF MY BLUE EYES

THE BEST OF ANNE KIRKPATRICK
ALL HE DID WAS TELL ME LIES
HOLD ON ME
DARLIN' PAL OF MINE
ONLY LOVE CAN BREAK A HEART
TAKE ME HOME
SAILING
I KNOW A HEARTACHE

49

UPROAR
LONG AGO SHOES
STANDING TOO CLOSE TO THE FLAME
COME BACK AGAIN
SAFE IN THE ARMS OF LOVE
GOULBURN STREET
MERRY-GO-ROUND OF LIFE
THE LAME FIDDLER
ANECDOTES OF YOU
MY TOWN
TONIGHT I'LL SHOOT THE MOON
BABY WITH YOU
HONKY TONK GIRL

COME BACK AGAIN
I GOT YOU
SAFE IN THE ARMS OF LOVE
LONG AGO SHOES
LIGHTS IN THE MIRROR
BABY WITH YOU
HONKY TONK GIRL
COME BACK AGAIN
BORN FOR THE NIGHT LIFE
CARELESS HEART
SOMEBODY LOVES YOU
TAKE ME HOME
IN THE COUNTRY

CRY LIKE A MAN
YOU CAN BELIEVE IN ME
MANY MOTHERS
GOIN' STRONG, GOIN' WRONG
ARE YOU WASTING MY TIME
CHANGE YOUR NAME
SHE'S GOIN' AGAIN
THE HEART OF THE LAND
OLD HOME TOWN
HIT AND RUN
CRY LIKE A MAN
FOREVER NEVER FELT SO FAR AWAY
THAT'S ALL YOU EVER GOT FROM ME

DOWN HOME
JOHN HARDY
HOMESTEAD BLUES
LONG BLACK VEIL
LOUISE
HONKY TONK BLUES
DARLING PAL OF MINE
WE'LL SWEEP OUT THE ASHES IN THE MORNING
BURY ME BENEATH THE WILLOW
TRAIN LEAVES HERE THIS MORNING
ONE DAY BLUES
I'M THINKING TONIGHT OF MY BLUE EYES
ONE ROSE

GAME OF LOVE
GAME OF LOVE
EASTBOUND TRAIN
ROULETTE WHEEL OF LOVE
HOLD'S TOO STRONG
CRADLE OF LOVE
CIRCLE CAFE
FROZEN EMOTION
HEARTBROKEN
AM I THE ONE
WHITES OF YOUR EYES
DON'T BLAME ME
A PLACE CALLED LONESOME

LET THE SONGS KEEP FLOWING STRONG & NATURALLY
HOLD ON ME
HAYES
ONLY LOVE CAN BREAK YOUR HEART
UPROAR
OLD AUNT ELISA
OLD PAL OF YESTERDAY
FEEL A WHOLE LOT BETTER
MY TOWN
I'M NOT LISA
RAINBOWS OVER YOUR BLUES
AS IF I DIDN'T KNOW
SEED OF MUSIC
TAKE MY HAND (WITH SLIM DUSTY ON ACOUSTIC GUITAR)

MERRY-GO-ROUND OF LIFE
GOULBURN STREET
MERRY-GO-ROUND OF LIFE
KNOCKIN' AROUND
LOVE FROM THE SIDELINES
MAMMAS DON'T LET YOUR BABIES GROW UP TO BE
COWBOYS
STANDING TOO CLOSE TO THE FLAME
RING OF FIRE
SWEET RAIN
THE LAME FIDDLER
BRAND NEW LOVE
WAITING FOR A TRAIN
YOUR LOVE'S NOT ENOUGH

OUT OF THE BLUE
I GUESS WE'VE BEEN TOGETHER FOR TOO LONG
TRAIN WRECK OF EMOTION
I DON'T GO BACK ANY MORE
TAKE YOUR TIME
A BOTTLE OF WINE AND PATSY CLINE
OUT OF THE BLUE
THE SAME MISTAKE
SIGHT FOR SORE EYES
BROKEN BLEEDING HURTIN' HEART
SWEET MOMENTS
THE DANCE
THERE GOES MY HEART AGAIN
GOODBYE

SHOOT THE MOON
SAILING
GRIEVOUS ANGEL
ALL HE DID WAS TELL ME LIES
ANNIE JOHNSON
LONESOME ME
ANECDOTES OF YOU
LADY WITH THE BRAID
FRENCH WALTZ
QUESTION
TONIGHT I'LL SHOOT THE MOON

EVERYBODY'S LOOKING FOR SOMETHING ON A SATURDAY
NIGHT
WITH INSERTS FROM:
SATURDAY NIGHT AT THE MOVIES
SAD MOVIES ALWAYS MAKE ME CRY
ANOTHER SATURDAY NIGHT
BOBBY'S GIRL

SHOWMAN'S DAUGHTER
SHOWMAN'S DAUGHTER
DRIVE AWAY
SILO'S OF HOME
NEVER SAY NEVER
WOMEN OF THE WEST
BLUER SKIES
THE CUNNAMULLA FELLER
PEPPIMENARTI CRADLE
GOODBYE
NEVERLAND
WHEN IT'S LAMPLIGHTING TIME IN THE VALLEY
WHEN THE RAIN TUMBLES DOWN IN JULY

ANNE KIRKPATRICK ANNETHOLOGY BONUS EDITION 2CD
DISC 1
GRIEVOUS ANGEL (2010 DIGITAL REMASTER)
HERE WE ARE (DUET WITH BILL CHAMBERS)
BORN FOR THE NIGHT LIFE (2010 DIGITAL REMASTER)
HONKY TONK (2010 DIGITAL REMASTER)
TRAVELLIN' STILL, ALWAYS WILL
TRAVELLIN' STILL, ALWAYS WILL
A BOTTLE OF WINE AND PATSY CLINE
FEEL A WHOLE LOT BETTER (2010 DIGITAL REMASTER
YOU AIN'T GOING NOWHERE (LIVE)
SIN CITY (LIVE)
I'M THINKING TONIGHT MY BLUE EYES (2010 DIGITAL
REMASTER)
COME BACK AGAIN (2010 DIGITAL REMASTER)
YOU CAN BELIEVE IN ME (2010 DIGITAL REMASTER)
MANY MOTHERS (2010 DIGITAL REMASTER)
OLD SUNLANDER VAN (2010 DIGITAL REMASTER)
BURY ME BENEATH THE WILLOW (LIVE)
EASTBOUND TRAIN

ALL HE DID WAS TELL ME LIES (2010 DIGITAL REMASTER)
STILL COMING DOWN FROM YOU (2010 DIGITAL REMATSER)
SAFE IN THE ARMS OF LOVE (2010 DIGITAL REMASTER)
PEPPIMENARTI CRADLE
SHOWMAN'S DAUGHTER
LAST DRIVE
DISC 2: BONUS ALBUM - OUT OF THE BLUE
I GUESS WE'VE BEEN TOGETHER FOR TOO LONG
TRAINWRECK OF EMOTION
I DON'T GO BACK ANYMORE
TAKE YOUR TIME
A BOTTLE OF WINE AND PATSY CLINE
OUT OF THE BLUE
THE SAME MISTAKE
SIGHT FOR SORE EYES
BROKEN BLEEDING HURTING HEART
SWEET MOMENTS; THE DANCE
THERE GOES MY HEART AGAIN
GOODBYE

SINGLES
ALL HE DID WAS TELL ME LIES (VINYL)
BROKEN BLEEDING HURTIN' HEART (CD)
COME BACK AGAIN (VINYL)
FOOL'S GOLD RING (VINYL)
GAME OF LOVE (CD)
LOVE'S OLD SONG (VINYL)
MANY MOTHERS (CD)
MERRY-GO-ROUND OF LIFE (VINYL)
OUT OF THE BLUE (VINYL)
SAFE IN THE ARMS OF LOVE (VINYL)
STILL COMING DOWN FROM YOU (VINYL)
TRAIN LEAVES HERE THIS MORNING (VINYL)
TRAIN WRECK OF EMOTION (VINYL)
TRAVELLIN' STILL ...ALWAYS WILL (CD)

BIBLIOGRAPHY

Kasey Chambers:
All the Albums were found at
http://store.countrymusic.com.au/store/item.inetstore?id=3332K
ASEY DVD MAX

Melinda Schneider:
All the Albums were found at:
http://www.lyricsmania.com/melinda_schneider_lyrics.html

Beccy Cole:
All the Albums were found at:
http://www.cduniverse.com/search/xx/music/artist/Cole,+Beccy/
a/Beccy+Cole.htm

Felicity Urquhart:
Cover Picture Courtesy Rebecca McCarth Rum Entertainment
All the Albums were found at:
http://www.cduniverse.com/search/xx/music/artist/Felicity+Urq
uhart/a/albums.htm

Tania Kernaghan:
Cover Picture Courtesy Karen Waters PA to Tania Kernaghan
All the Albums were found at:
http://www.cduniverse.com/productinfo.asp?pid=6946730

Anne Kirkpatrick:
All the Albums were found at:
http://store.countrymusic.com.au/store/list.inetstore?id=30

ABOUT THE AUTHOR

I was 59 years old; a mother of three very special and supportive adult children and a grandmother of three wonderful grandsons (I now have five grand-children.) when I started writing my first book whilst watching a Bon Jovi concert DVD. (I am an avid fan, if you can call me that; crazy is more like it.)

I write from the heart and I really enjoyed writing the book so I wrote another using a different artist, and the books kept coming to me and I kept writing them.(with a little help from above)

Because I use different artist/artists song titles, I have to be very careful with Copyright so a lot of legal requirements have to be taken into consideration before publishing the books. I also needed a name that would connect my books to each other; so the "Song Title Series" books began.

All my books are short stories; however it depends on how many song titles there are to be used, as to the length of the book. Some artists didn't have enough song titles on their own so I combined them with a few other artists. Other artists had that many song titles that I could have written a novel; but it would have ended up being boring.

Challenges I like, so writing books with various artists are a lot of fun and require careful thinking.

Why should I have all the fun writing the books and not be able to share them with everyone; so I have converted them into large print books and E-Books so that you can share my fun as well.

Hopefully in the not too distant future; the books will also be available as audio books so that no-one will miss out on my fun and enjoyment of writing these unique books. I hope that you enjoy reading them.

My web site www.songtitleseries.com is the place to visit for updates of new books and a place to purchase other titles in other formats.

TESTIMONIALS

Joan has come up with a really unique concept with this 'Song Title Series"
I found this book interesting, and was fascinated at the way she has included so many song titles into the story.
It's a great read and something a little different from most novels.
Adam Harvey (Australian Country Music Artist)

"Having read three of the Song Title Series, all in the Country Music field, I found them to be a very interesting and refreshing change to the usual books that I read.
Joan has written them very well, and has used loads of imagination and cleverness to make them very unique! Very impressive!!"
Colleen B.
Tamworth (Country Music Capital)

After reading through your range of books I felt I must compliment you Joan on the imaginative and entertaining way in which you presented each group and the Musicians in those groups. The way the stories were constructed is a credit to your work ethic. These must have taken considerable time to piece together and it is obviously a work of love for you.
I wish you all the success you truly deserve and look forward to seeing you next time you visit Tamworth.
Peter Harkins
Managing Director Cheapa Music
Country Music Capital Tamworth

The song titles series are books that were intriguing and were hard to believe that these short stories were written within the incorporated song titles of the artists that are mentioned in the titles. I loved what I have read so far and think that anyone with an imagination and love of music as the author you will surely enjoy reading these.
L.K. Brisbane Australia.

Joan Maguire Books are very nice, I enjoy reading them so much, they are hard to put down!! Especially when she does one about Bonjovi and their songs!!! If I can say, it is worth every penny, when you buy one!!! The Books make nice presents, for a person whom loves to read!!! I can guarantee that you will LOVE these books, because I do!!!!!!!!!
Dawn from Newark, Delaware in the United States of America

I am Susie and would like to tell you guys, how much I am enjoying Joan Maguire's Books!! They are very enjoyable, and they are something that you do not ever want to put down!! I really enjoy these books; I can't wait until the next one that she puts out!!!!!!! I say go to your local book store, today and get one, you will not be disappointed!!!!!
Sue-from the United States of America

www.ingramcontent.com/pod-product-compliance
Lightning Source LLC
Chambersburg PA
CBHW060201070426
42447CB00033B/2257